Scott Joplin (1867? – 1917), "The King of Ragtime", wrote 44 original ragtime pieces, one ragtime ballet, and two operas. One of his first pieces, the Maple Leaf Rag, became ragtime's first and most influential hit, and has been recognized as the archetypal rag. He was born into a musical African American family of laborers in Northeast Texas, and developed his musical knowledge with the help of local teachers, most notably Julius Weiss. While growing up in Texarkana he formed a vocal quartet, and taught mandolin and guitar. During the late 1880s he left his job as a laborer with the railroad, and travelled around the American South as an itinerant musician. He went to Chicago for the World's Fair of 1893, which played a major part in making ragtime a national craze by 1897. In 1894 he moved to Sedalia, Missouri, and earned a living teaching piano and going on tour across the Southern US. During this period he taught future ragtime composers Arthur Marshall, Scott Hayden and Brun Campbell. Joplin began publishing music in 1895, and publication of his Maple Leaf Rag in 1899 brought him fame and had a profound influence on subsequent writers of ragtime. It also brought the composer a steady income for life. During his lifetime, Joplin did not reach this level of success again and frequently had financial problems. In 1901 he moved to St. Louis where he continued to compose and publish music, and regularly performed in brothels and bars in the city's red-light district. By the time he had moved to St. Louis, Joplin may have been experiencing discoordination of the fingers, tremors, and an inability to speak clearly, as a result of having contracted syphilis. The score to his first opera, A Guest of Honor, was confiscated in 1903 with his belongings due to his non-payment of bills, and is considered lost. He continued to compose and publish music, and in 1907 moved to New York City, seeking to find a producer for a new opera. He attempted to go beyond the limitations of the musical form which made him famous, without much monetary success. His second opera, Treemonisha, was not received well at its partially staged performance in 1915. In 1916, suffering from tertiary syphilis and by consequence rapidly deteriorating health, Joplin descended into dementia. He was admitted to a mental institution in January 1917, and died there three months later at the age of 49.

"The Cascades"

KEY SHEET & STAGING

Drum Set

KICK BASS   STICK OVER RIM   TOM TOM   CRASH CYM

SNARE   WOODBLOCK   CLOSED HI HAT   SPLASH CYM

STAGING RECOMMENDATION:

DRUM SET

VIBRAPHONE

MARIMBA 1   MARIMBA 2

XYLOHONE

-----------------------STAGE FRONT---------------------

"The Cascades"
A Rag for Mallet Quartet

Scott Joplin
Ed Argenziano

Score

(♩ = 120)

5

"The Cascades"

"The Cascades"

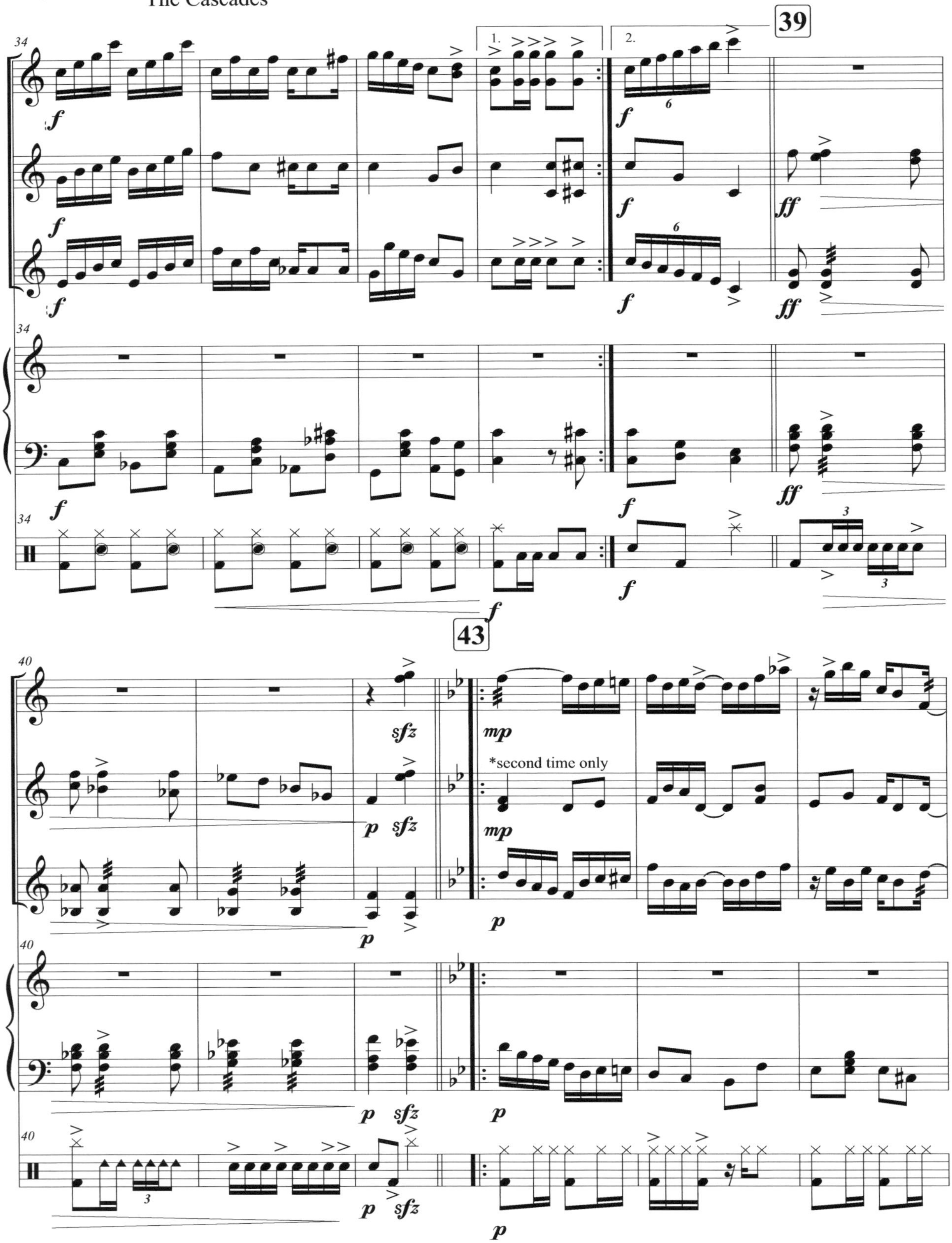
Xyl.
Vib.
Mrb.
Mrb.
D. S.
39
43
*second time only

"The Cascades"

56
Xyl.
Vib.
Mrb.
Mrb.
D. S.
1.
2.
60
p–ff
p–ff
p–ff
p–ff
mf
mf
p–ff
3
62
Xyl.
Vib.
Mrb.
Mrb.
D. S.

"The Cascades"

"The Cascades"
A Rag for Mallet Quartet

Xylophone

Scott Joplin
Ed Argenziano

"The Cascades"

"The Cascades"
A Rag for Mallet Quartet

Scott Joplin
Ed Argenziano

Vibraphone

"The Cascades"

"The Cascades"

"The Cascades"
A Rag for Mallet Quartet

Marimba 1

Scott Joplin
Ed Argenziano

"The Cascades"

"The Cascades"

Marimba 2

"The Cascades"
A Rag for Mallet Quartet

Scott Joplin
Ed Argenziano

2   "The Cascades"

"The Cascades"

Drum Set

"The Cascades"

A Rag for Mallet Quartet

Scott Joplin
Ed Argenziano

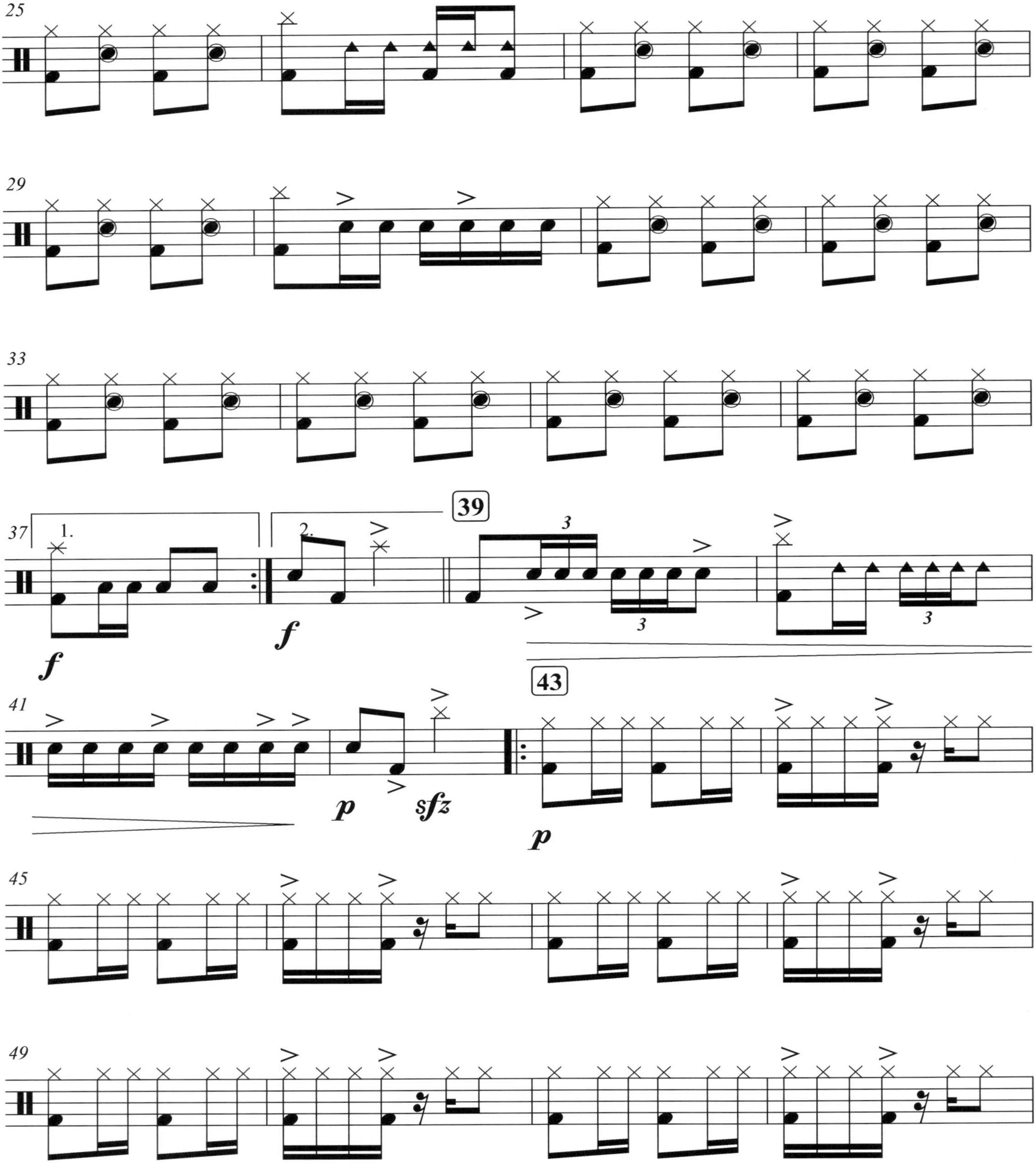
25
29
33
37
1.
2.
39
f
f
3
3
3
41
43
p
sfz
p
45
49

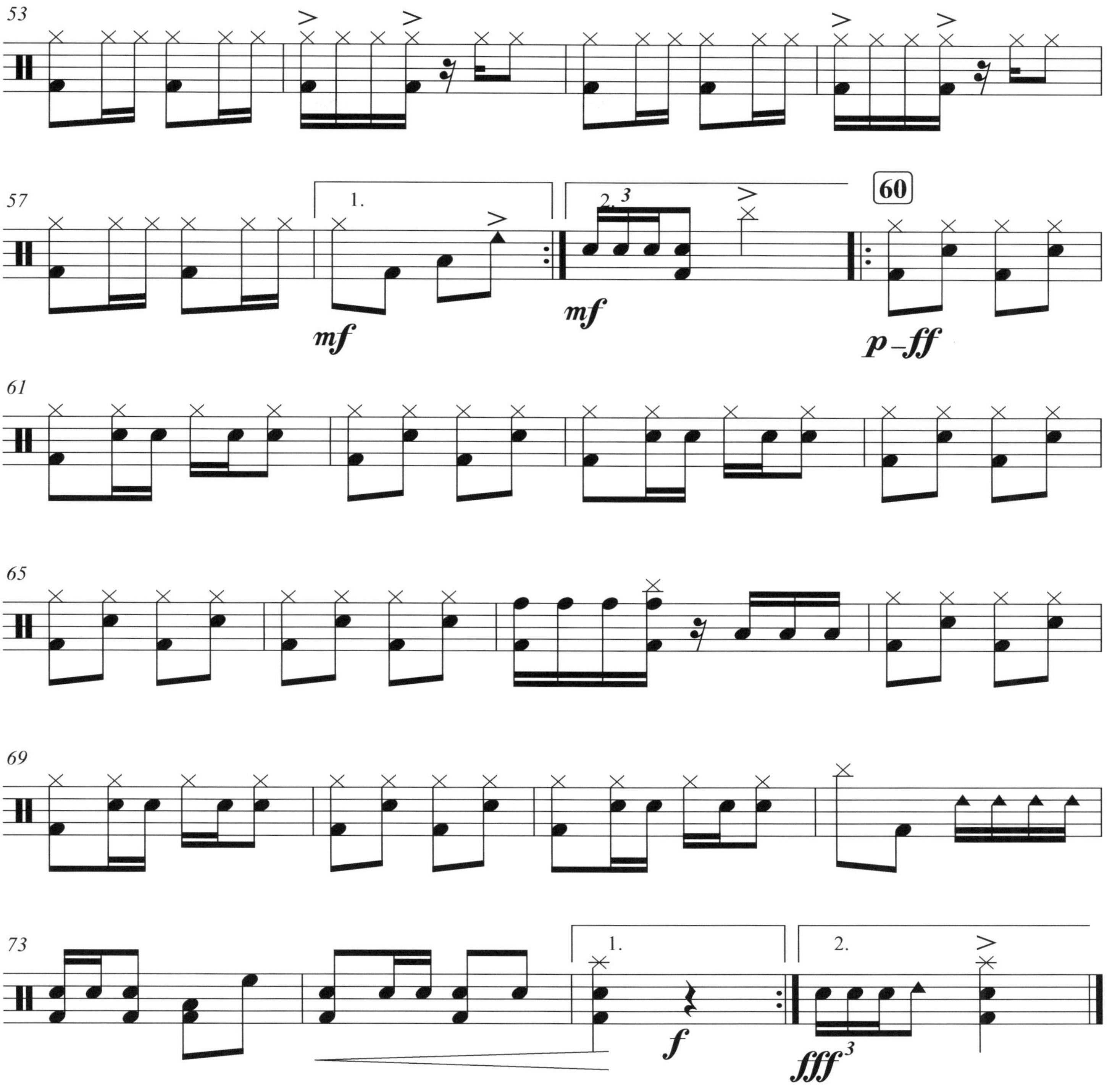
53
57
1.
2.
mf
mf
60
p–ff
61
65
69
73
1.
2.
f
fff

About the author...

Edward Argenziano presently lives in Clearwater, Florida. He holds a Bachelor of Science Degree in Music Education from William Paterson University and a Masters of Arts Degree in Music Performance from Montclair State University. He began playing the drums at the age of five, and he continues to hold a deep passion for this instrument to this day.

Ed has been a secondary school teacher in New Jersey and Florida for 32 years. In this role, he was the Fine Arts Department Chairperson & Director of Bands and Orchestras at Clearwater High School in Clearwater, FL and Director of Bands and Orchestra at Morris Knolls High School in Rockaway, NJ. He also served as a music composition middle college teacher for Fairleigh Dickinson University.

While in New Jersey, Ed served as the North Jersey Area Honors Band President and Conductor and New Jersey Allstate Percussion coordinator. He has 34 years of experience coordinating and adjudicating District, Area, Region and Allstate Band percussion auditions for many years.

Since 1987, Ed has been extremely involved as a music/percussion clinician and music adjudicator and has toured extensively throughout the United States, Canada, Europe, and Japan. Presently, he is judging music for W.G.I. Percussion, Bands of America, and Drum Corps International. Currently, he is also an Educational Artist for the Zildjian Cymbal Company, Vic Firth Drum Company, REMO Percussion, and Ludwig/Musser Company.

You can check out his numerous percussion arrangements and compositions at www.edargenziano.com. Many of his pieces have been performed throughout the world.

Made in the USA
Las Vegas, NV
11 September 2021